CONTENTS

Urbanization in China's Lower Yangzi Delta

Transactional Relations and the Repositioning of Locality

EAI Occasional Paper No. 10

Urbanization in China's Lower Yangzi Delta

Transactional Relations and the Repositioning of Locality

Andrew M. Marton

EAST ASIAN INSTITUTE
National University of Singapore

World Scientific
Singapore • New Jersey • London • Hong Kong

SINGAPORE UNIVERSITY PRESS
NATIONAL UNIVERSITY OF SINGAPORE

Published by

World Scientific Publishing Co. Pte. Ltd.
P O Box 128, Farrer Road, Singapore 912805
USA office: Suite 1B, 1060 Main Street, River Edge, NJ 07661
UK office: 57 Shelton Street, Covent Garden, London WC2H 9HE

and

Singapore University Press Pte. Ltd.
Yusof Ishak House, National University of Singapore
10 Kent Ridge Crescent, Singapore 119260

URBANIZATION IN CHINA'S LOWER YANGZI DELTA:
Transactional Relations and the Repositioning of Locality
EAI OCCASIONAL PAPER No. 10

ISBN 981-02-3757-X (pbk)

Printed in Singapore.

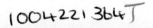

URBANIZATION IN CHINA'S LOWER YANGZI DELTA: TRANSACTIONAL RELATIONS AND THE REPOSITIONING OF LOCALITY

Andrew M. MARTON

URBANIZATION IN CHINA'S LOWER YANGZI DELTA: TRANSACTIONAL RELATIONS AND THE REPOSITIONING OF LOCALITY

Andrew M. MARTON [#]

The development of market socialism in China has contributed to a remarkable spatial economic transformation in particular areas of the Chinese countryside. The conventional wisdom of existing theories of urban transition does not adequately explain the emergence of these open textured landscapes of mixed agricultural and non-agricultural activities. This paper examines some of the key processes and mechanisms of regional restructuring in one county level jurisdiction in the lower Yangzi delta. A case study of Kunshan situates the emergence of specific patterns of industrial production within a complex network of interactions and interrelationships embedded in overlapping administrative and institutional structures which are themselves largely tied to the circumstances of particular places. Two central findings are revealed. First, the patterns and underlying processes and mechanisms of regional development in the delta are fundamentally linked to intensely localized exigencies and opportunities within the wider space economy. Second, external economies, the dynamics of agglomeration, and the role of large cities and

[#] Dr. Andrew Marton is a Research Fellow in the East Asian Institute. The author wishes to thank Professor John Wong who offered constructive criticism of an earlier draft of this paper.

other exogenous forces, while significant, were less important in the delta than were endogenous forces. Highlighted are a number of issues which need to be accommodated in a new conceptual framework for understanding and explaining urbanization in China's lower Yangzi delta. The paper concludes by outlining a planning and management agenda which responds to the resulting conceptual and analytical shift in emphasis.

Introduction

China's distinctive experience of socialist transition in a partially marketizing economy serves as a unique rubric for examining the critical processes and mechanisms of rural-urban transformation in Asia. Perhaps the most important reason for paying attention to the socialist transition in China, however, is the truly intriguing and unique patterns and processes of growth and development which have emerged during the reform period since 1978. Chief among these, was the apparent capacity to rapidly industrialize without transferring large numbers of people into big cities. One of the most striking elements of this transition has been the phenomenal growth and spatial proliferation of industries in the Chinese countryside. The opening up of markets and the increasing autonomy of enterprises with reforms has entailed an erosion of the divisions between rural and urban, reflected in the emergence of particular patterns of settlement and economic activity, which conform clearly to neither. The key assertion of this paper is that understanding and explaining processes of spatial economic transformation in China must involve a more subtle analysis of the interplay between local circumstances and macro-forces than has hitherto been apparent.

Several recent commentaries have highlighted the way in which theories of urban transformation must reposition locality, considered variously in terms of culture, history and the socio-economic and political circumstances of place, within the broader context of regional development.[1] Even in the context of accelerated globalization of modern industry, the local and regional dimensions of economic activity have become accentuated.[2] Localized and regional economic "communities" as Storper and Scott have suggested, embody certain dynamics that attach to the places in which they develop and which constitute a place-specific economic culture and its underlying structures.

As development is increasingly seen as a localized phenomenon, this augurs for a commensurate shift in the intellectual and analytical focus of inquiry. Rather than treating the region as a convenient neutral backdrop for spatial change, there needs to be a greater commitment to probing the dynamics of the processes of regional formation as they articulate with those changes. Ultimately, understanding rural-urban transformation in China requires conceptualizing the underlying processes and mechanisms in the context of local geographical and historical circumstances which at once shape and reflect the character of regions. The old unitary hierarchy of command relations under China's regime of central planning, which relied upon distinct administrative and economic boundaries between rural and urban, has yielded to modes of interaction which utilized a more vigorously diverse array of manipulation, concessions, coercion and partnerships. Changes in the structure of ownership also meant that increasingly independent economic actors in a restructuring space-economy were

---

[1] Douglass, M. (1995) Viewpoint; Bringing culture in: Locality and global capitalism in East Asia. *Third world planning review 17* (3), pp. iii–ix; McGee, T. G. (1995) Geography and development: Crisis commitment and renewal. *Cahiers de géographie du Québec 39* (108), pp. 527–536; Marton, A. M. (1995) Mega-urbanization in southern Jiangsu: Enterprise location and the reconstitution of local space. *Chinese environment and development. 6* (1–2), pp. 9–42; Massey, D. (1993) Questions of locality. *Geography 78* (2), pp. 142–149.

[2] Storper, M. & Scott, A. J. (1993) *The wealth of regions: Market forces and policy imperatives in local and global context.* Working Paper No. 7, Los Angeles: UCLA.

negotiating and managing their own mutually beneficial interactions and inter-relationships.

This paper will explore the relationships between the changing structure of community administration, the development of rural non-agricultural enterprises, and the emergence of institutional structures which managed local economic activity in Kunshan in the heart of China's lower Yangzi delta. Kunshan is a county level municipality (*xianji shi*) located in southern Jiangsu adjacent to the Shanghai Municipal region (see Figure 1). The centre of Kunshan is located 55 kilometres from downtown Shanghai and 36 kilometres from the city of Suzhou. Comprised of 20 towns and 466 villages, Kunshan covers an area of 865 square kilometres, 60.8 percent of which was cultivated land in 1996, with another 22.3 percent containing lakes, rivers and canals. At the end of 1996 the population was 583,364. The average annual growth rate of industrial output in Kunshan between 1979 and 1996 was 32.7 percent.[3] The emergence of non-agricultural activities in the Kunshan countryside since 1979 is also reflected in the declining proportion of the total value of output attributed to farming. Agriculture accounted for more than 35 percent of total output in Kunshan in 1979, decreasing to about 6 percent in 1996. The contribution of the tertiary sector rose from 13 percent to more than 17 percent over the same period.[4] As a result of this structural shift in the local economy, by 1996, per-capita GDP in Kunshan had reached RMB 19,660, nearly double that for the nearby city of Suzhou.[5]

---

[3] *Jiangsu Sishinian 1949–1989 (Jiangsu Forty Years 1949–1989)* Beijing: State Statistical Publishers, pp. 393–394; *Kunshan tongji nianjian [Several years] (Kunshan Statistical Yearbook)*. Kunshan: Kunshan Statistical Publishers; *Suzhou tongji nianjian 1997 (Suzhou Statistical Yearbook 1997)*. Beijing: State Statistical Publishers, p. 12.

[4] *Jiangsu sishinian 1949–1989 (Jiangsu Forty Years 1949–1989) op. cit.*, pp. 382, 394, 398; *Kunshan tongji nianjian 1996 (Kunshan Statistical Yearbook 1996). op. cit.*, p. 17.

[5] *Suzhou tongji nianjian 1997 (Suzhou Statistical Yearbook 1997). op. cit.*, pp. 40, 41, 46.

Figure 1

EAST CHINA, THE LOWER YANGZI DELTA, AND KUNSHAN, 1996

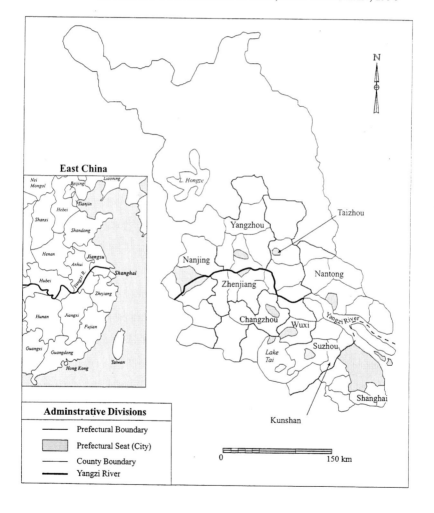

In addition to the conspicuousness and rapid pace of economic change, Kunshan's location and its administrative position in the lower Yangzi delta were appropriate for an evaluation of a range of potential forces which might have influenced the patterns and processes of this change. While Kunshan was located between and adjacent to two large urban centres, it was also administratively distinct and more independent than other areas lower in the administrative hierarchy. Kunshan was also topographically uniform and, as well as straddling major regional and national transportation corridors, had its own well-developed internal transportation network. Thus, Kunshan provides a quintessential example of the local character of regional change.

The following section introduces an alternative approach to understanding the underlying processes of this regional change in the lower Yangzi delta. It also positions the subsequent analysis in the context of local circumstances as they articulate with the wider space economy. The next section reviews recent changes in community administration in Kunshan and how these were related to the wider hierarchy of authority and jurisdiction in China. This part also discusses how reforms in public finances stimulated local development imperatives and the emergence of rural industrial enterprises. The third section examines how the spatial proliferation of enterprises is related to these issues. Details of how community governments in Kunshan formalized local institutional structures and the means by which local cadres were able to influence town and village development are discussed in the fourth section. The fifth section highlights the key elements of spatial change in the lower Yangzi delta to illustrate how the changing structure of community government, the emergence of local institutional structures, and their relationship to spatial economic transformation challenge conventional views of regional development in China. A framework which conceptualizes and links the critical local elements of this transformation to generalizations about the wider regional patterns and trends will also be suggested. The paper concludes by outlining a planning and management agenda in response to this conceptual and analytical shift in emphasis.

Urbanization, the Transactional Environment, and Local Circumstances

Writing in an advanced, Western, capitalist economy context, regional economies as conceived of by Storper and Scott, typically faced certain "endemic failures and crisis tendencies".[6] This is quite contrary to the apparent success of regional industrial complexes in China which have increasingly emerged outside the more conventional urban forms. However, Storper and Scott also allude to the analytical and conceptual tools for understanding why this is so. They emphasize how regional industrial formation relies on a kind of industrial culture and its inherent sub-structures of interactions and inter-relationships. These structures embody networks of transactions, broadly conceived, which sustain processes of economic, political and social relations.

While spatial scientists have established the main categories of these interactions and interrelationships, focusing on the identification and measurement of flows is often difficult, and in any case, addresses only part of a very complex picture. It is necessary, therefore, to adopt an approach which focuses instead upon the conditions which create such interactions and the circumstances within which they exist. The notion of a "transactional environment" is introduced here to capture this broader perspective. "Transactional" refers to the now standard framework of interactions and interrelationships initially proposed by Preston and elaborated upon by Rondinelli and Unwin: migration; flows of goods, services, energy and technological and social information; financial transfers and the transfer of capital in other

---

[6] Storper & Scott (1993) *op. cit.*, p. 1.

forms; and other transactional activities.[7] "Environment" refers to overlapping structural, organizational, and social relationships and interdependencies including: political and administrative imperatives and hierarchies; legal and regulatory frameworks; patterns of jurisdiction, decision-making and power; socio-economic exigencies and opportunities, and all their various transactional networks. Taken together these elements comprise a transactional environment, the analysis of which can provide insights into the mechanisms and processes that underlie regional change.

Conventional views of the transactional structure of a production system tend to focus on transaction costs ignoring the local institutional context and the detailed character of enterprises. An examination of the transactional environment, on the other hand, necessarily combines analysis of micro-scale decision patterns of enterprises, their institutional and transactive contexts, and place-specific socio-cultural and political-economic particularities to explain patterns and processes of regional economic development. In this context, the nature of transactional activities of enterprises in and of themselves are as important as their production activities. Thus, not only are the interactions and inter-relationships which constitute the transactional environment constructed over space, but they are also largely determined by, and embedded within the unique intersection of circumstances which constitute place. This is most clearly demonstrated in the spatial proliferation of industrial activity in the lower Yangzi

---

[7] Preston, D. (1975) Rural-urban and inter-settlement interaction: Theory and analytical structure. *Area 7* (3), pp. 171–174; Rondinelli, D. A. (1983) *Secondary cities in developing countries: Policies for diffusing urbanization*. Beverly Hills: Sage; Rondinelli, D. A. (1985) *Applied methods of regional analysis: The spatial dimensions of development policy*. Boulder: Westview; Unwin, T. (1989) Urban-rural interaction in developing countries: A theoretical perspective. In Potter, R. B. & Unwin, T. (Eds.) *The geography of urban-rural interaction in developing countries*. London: Routledge, pp. 11–32.

delta. While cities are commonly viewed as the nexus of growth, regional development in the delta appears to be more complex than merely in terms of its purported dependence upon urban centred forces.[8]

The critical parameters and the vitality of regional development in the lower Yangzi delta were in fact centred within the multitude of localities, fundamentally challenging the conventionally perceived role of large cities. Moreover, while the importance of agricultural production has not diminished in terms of the output of staple grains, new roles in industrial production and other non-agricultural activities have emerged that create locally specific opportunities for accumulation making rural areas the foci for socio-economic transformation. The unit area yield of staple grains in Kunshan, for example, was 7000 kg/hectare in 1996, 56 percent more than the national average. Meanwhile, non-urban per-capita values for gross industrial output and GDP in places like Kunshan equaled or exceeded comparable indices for nearby cities such as Suzhou and Shanghai.[9] It is striking that the lower Yangzi delta can retain its national prominence as China's premier agricultural producer region, while at the same time undergoing rapid industrial growth. It would seem there are aspects of the delta's transactional environment not fully captured in the conventional explanations of the dynamics of regional industrial expansion and urbanization.

---

[8] On this point see: Kwok, R. Y. W. (1992) Urbanization under economic reform. In Guldin, G. E. (Ed.) *Urbanizing China*. Westport: Greenwood, p. 73, and; Pannell, C. W. (1992) The role of great cities in China. In Guldin, G. E. (Ed.) *op. cit.*, p. 36, both of whom claim that rural industrial development is incapable of taking place independently of large cities or of being self generated.

[9] *Shanghai tongji nianjian 1997* (*Shanghai Statistical Yearbook 1997*). Beijing: State Statistical Publishers, p. 5; *Suzhou tongji nianjian 1997* (*Suzhou Statistical Yearbook 1997*). *op. cit.*, pp. 40, 41, 46, 76, 78.

The transactional environment is mediated through a number of formal and informal administrative and institutional parameters. These are linked to bifurcation of the role of local governments (discussed below) both as community administrators and as owners and managers of non-agricultural enterprises. Within the transactional environment, processes of representation embedded in various administrative and institutional structures allow for the local mobilization of indigenous and external means of production. These locally determined representations manipulate the transactional networks, sometimes creating new ones, in order to maximize community-based production opportunities. In the absence of a meaningful legal and regulatory framework localities are free to exploit all means at their disposal to achieve this objective. Local actors, often with apparently conflicting roles, exercise their influence through these intensely localized economic and bureaucratic structures. This helps to explain the intensity and diffuse nature of local transactional networks, both within structures and across space.

These networks of transactions, and their underlying interactions and interrelationships, are embedded and manifest in local and regional institutional structures which have emerged to manage, negotiate and manipulate local economic activity. The processes by which institutional structures are linked to regional economic development in China are complex, usually ill-defined, and frequently quite puzzling. By undertaking an analysis that is sensitive to local cultural and historical circumstances, however, particular insights can reveal how spatial economic change is affected by evolving institutional structures, and conversely, uncover the socio-political consequences of recent reforms and the resulting transformation within China's rapidly developing regions. Understanding and explaining the precise spatial patterns within such regions in China rests upon a detailed examination of the local and regional institutional structures, as they relate to both the larger patterns and trends of spatial-economic transformation, and more specifically to the activities of industrial enterprises within their institutional and transactive contexts.

Bifurcation of the Functions of Local Government

Community Administration

On July 27, 1989 Kunshan was administratively reclassified from a county (*xian*) to a county level city (*xianji shi*). Having met certain criteria which accorded it economically more developed status, the new designation was intended to promote further industrialization and urban construction. The inclusion of large areas of the Kunshan countryside into "city" status (the former county boundary remained unchanged) was aimed at better integrating rural and urban sectors at the local level. Able to deal more directly with the province, Kunshan also experienced less interference from intermediate levels of administration since, with reclassification, it became equal in planning terms to the prefectural level city of Suzhou. This increased autonomy included greater authority to collect and retain tax revenues from enterprises and to locally approve higher values of external investment in Kunshan. More than anything else, local authorities emphasized how "city" status carried greater prestige than the county designation. Since Kunshan became "more famous", outsiders would be more willing to invest here, and as a city, they could set higher standards for themselves.

Kunshan's city designation also changed its internal relationship with its 20 townships, the lowest level of the urban administrative hierarchy. By 1990 all 20 had been elevated from township (*xiang*) to designated town (*jianzhi zhen*) status. As with the county level reclassification, designated towns in Kunshan acquired new authority to raise funds for local development. In addition, they were also supposed to receive county (now city) level allocations for town construction. In practice, however, these funds were inadequate, so town governments increasingly turned to other more substantial and stable sources of revenue. Under the official notion of "town leading the development of the countryside", towns were to act as a "bridge" to revenue generating opportunities in areas of the countryside directly under their jurisdiction.[10]

Figure 2 illustrates the location of town seats, their respective administrative regions, and Kunshan's 466 villages. Village level administrative boundaries are not shown. In addition to their respective government functions, Yushan and Chengbei town seats formed the built-up core of Kunshan, including the municipal (Kunshan) government seat, and were administered as a single urban unit by the Kunshan level bureaucracy. The municipal government also directly administered at least five specialized state farms in Zhoushi, Zhengyi, and Penglang towns, the Special Economic and Technological Development Zone straddling Yushan and Lujia towns, and the Red Flag (*Hong Qi*) Industrial Area in Bacheng, jointly administered with Yushan. While the administrative boundaries illustrated in Figure 2 were spatially distinct, they also embodied complex overlapping, and often conflicting, patterns of authority, jurisdiction, and power that were much less clear. This was true not only of different levels in the administrative hierarchy, but also of the various agencies at any given level. Understanding the nature of how these patterns were constructed, negotiated, and operationalized in Kunshan reveals much about the processes and characteristics of local development. Before proceeding, however, it is necessary to provide an administrative context over and through which such patterns emerged.

---

[10] Interview notes.

Figure 2

KUNSHAN: ADMINISTRATIVE DIVISIONS, 1997

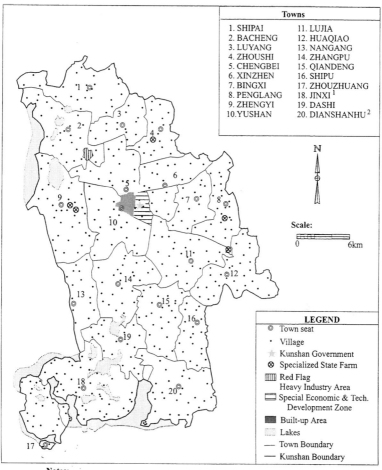

Towns	
1. SHIPAI	11. LUJIA
2. BACHENG	12. HUAQIAO
3. LUYANG	13. NANGANG
4. ZHOUSHI	14. ZHANGPU
5. CHENGBEI	15. QIANDENG
6. XINZHEN	16. SHIPU
7. BINGXI	17. ZHOUZHUANG
8. PENGLANG	18. JINXI [1]
9. ZHENGYI	19. DASHI
10.YUSHAN	20. DIANSHANHU [2]

N

Scale:

0   6km

LEGEND	
◎	Town seat
•	Village
✶	Kunshan Government
⊗	Specialized State Farm
▥	Red Flag
	Heavy Industry Area
▭	Special Economic & Tech. Development Zone
■	Built-up Area
▦	Lakes
—	Town Boundary
—	Kunshan Boundary

Notes:
1. Formerly Chenmu
2. Formerly Diandong

Table 1 outlines the structure and development of the Kunshan administration between 1978 and 1995. Only the main units of local government in Kunshan are listed. Excluded are the numerous sub-sections and subordinate offices of the local bureaucracy. Also excluded are the chief decision-making and executive bodies sitting atop these bureaux, the various organs of the Chinese Communist Party (CCP), and grassroots organizations such as the Political Consultative Committee, and the local Congress of People's Deputies. The table illustrates, therefore, changes in the broad mid-level administration of the local government bureaucracy. The first two columns for 1978 and 1985 illustrate the changes which occurred between the late 1970s when central planning remained dominant to the mid-1980s by which time the reforms had become well established. The last column for 1995 outlines the most recent elements of community administration in the period often referred to as "market socialism". Two fundamental trends are apparent. The first is the enormous expansion in the size and range of responsibilities of the local bureaucracy since 1978. The second might be described as the corporatization of the bureaucratic-administrative mid-section of the Kunshan government. Both trends were linked to the disengagement of the central government from local administration and the reduction of state allocations which financed many of its functions. Thus, while central and provincial authorities still determined local obligations through economic and administrative policies and regulations, their financing and implementation at the county level and below were a largely local enterprise.

The term "enterprise" is here used deliberately to connote the way in which local government in Kunshan bifurcated into the dual roles of community administrator, and owner and manager of several companies and corporate-like economic entities. Table 1 lists only a few of these. In 1996 there were at least 120 companies directly or indirectly affiliated with some part of the Kunshan level government bureaucracy. Some of these firms emerged as a result of the partial

Table 1

STRUCTURE AND DEVELOPMENT OF COMMUNITY ADMINISTRATION IN KUNSHAN, 1978–1995

1978 (Central Planning)	1985 (Reform)	1995 (Market Socialism)
County Government Office	County Government Office	Municipal Government Office[1]
Civil Affairs Bureau	Civil Affairs Bureau	Civil Affairs Bureau[1]
		Civil Affairs Industrial Company
		Administrative Organs Mgmt. Bureau
Culture and Education Bureau	Culture and Education Bureau	Culture Bureau
		Education Bureau
		School Industries Supply and Sales Sectn.
Personnel Bureau	Personnel Bureau	Personnel Bureau[1]
	Labour Bureau	Labour Bureau
		Labour Services Company
		Employment Management Office
	Statistics Bureau	Statistics Bureau
		Price Bureau
Financial Services Bureau	Financial Services Bureau	Finance Bureau
		Jiangsu and Suzhou Accounting Offices
		Audit Bureau
	Tax Bureau	Local Tax Bureau
		National Tax Bureau
Public Security Bureau	Public Security Bureau	Public Security Bureau
	Justice Bureau	Justice Bureau
Grain Bureau	Grain Bureau	Grain Bureau[1]
		Cereals & Edible Oils Sup. and Sales Co.
	Food Office	Food Company
Agriculture Bureau	Agriculture Bureau	Agriculture Bureau[1]

1978 (Central Planning)	1985 (Reform)	1995 (Market Socialism)
		Agricultural Products and Materials Co.
Water Conservancy Bureau	Water Conservancy Bureau	Water Conservancy Bureau
Agricultural Machinery Bureau		Agricultural Machinery Company[1]
Economic Diversification Mgmt. Bureau	Economic Diversification Mgmt. Bureau	Economic Diversification Mgmt. Bureau[1]
		Diversification Management Corporation[1]
		Sideline Products Office
Planning Committee	Planning Committee	Planning Commission
Industry Bureau	Industry and Commerce Bureau	Industry and Commerce Administration and Management Bureau
		Industry Supply and Sales Company
No. 2 Industry Bureau	Industrial Company	No. 2 Industrial Supply and Sales Co.
Commerce Bureau	Commerce Bureau	Commerce Bureau
Finance and Trade Office		Commercial Corporation
		Commercial Inspection Bureau
		Commercial Market Construction Office
Supply and Sales Office	Supply and Sales Office	Supply and Sales Cooperation Office
		Supply and Sales Corporation
Goods and Materials Bureau	Goods and Materials Bureau	Goods and Materials Bureau
		Goods and Materials Management Co.
		Coal and Petroleum Company
	Economic Commission	Economic Commission[1]
		Industrial Wholesale Company
		Chemical, Pharmaceutical and Construct. Materials Industries Bureau[1]

1978 (Central Planning)	1985 (Reform)	1995 (Market Socialism)

		Chemical and Pharmaceutical
		  Supply and Sales Company
		Construction Materials Co.
		Machinery, Electronics and
		  Metallurgical Industries
		  Bureau[1]
		Mach., Electronics, and
		  Metallurgical Co.
		Textiles Bureau[1]
		Textiles Company
		Light Industry Bureau
		Light Industry Company

	Rural Industry Bureau
	Economic Cooperation
	  Commission
		Rural Industry Bureau[1]
		Economic Cooperation
		  Commission[1]
		Economic and Technical
		  Cooperation Office
		Economic and Technical
		  Cooperation and
		  Development Company
		Poverty Alleviation
		  Development Office

		Economic System Reform Commission[1] Economic Research Centre[1]

Foreign Trade Bureau	Foreign Trade Bureau	Foreign Economic Relations
		  and Trade Commission
		Foreign Trade Company
		Suzhou Customs Office
		Special Economic and
		  Technological Dev Zone
		  (SETDZ) Mgmt. Committee[1]

		SETDZ Agriculture, Industry and Commercial Corp.

1978 (Central Planning)	1985 (Reform)	1995 (Market Socialism)
		Industrial Trade Corporation
		Tertiary Industry Office
		Tourism Bureau
		Economic Development Corporation
	Basic Construction Bureau	Urban and Rural Construction Bureau[1]
		Public Parks Construction Office
		Land Management Bureau
		Real Estate Development Administration
Public Health Bureau	Public Health Bureau	Public Health Bureau
Transportation Bureau	Transportation Bureau	Transportation Bureau[1]
		Transportation Corporation
Post and Telecommunications Bureau	Post and Telecommunications Bureau	Post and Telecommunications Bureau
Science Committee	Science and Technology Committee	Science and Technology Commission
Sports Committee	Sports Committee	Sports Committee
		Sanitation Committee
		Social Safety Management Committee
Birth Control Office	Birth Control Office	Birth Control Committee
		Standards and Measures Bureau
		Reception Bureau
		Investigations Bureau
	Nationalities and Religious Affairs Sectn.	Nationalities and Religious Affairs Sectn.
	Foreign Affairs Office	Foreign Affairs Office[1]
	Overseas Chinese Affairs Office	Overseas Chinese Affairs Office
		Overseas Chinese Construction Office

1978 (Central Planning)	1985 (Reform)	1995 (Market Socialism)
		Senior Citizens Office
	Archives Bureau	Archives Bureau
		Local Gazetteer Office
	Environmental Protection Office	Environmental Protection Bureau
		Environmental Protection Industry Supply and Sales Company
	Electricity Supply Bureau	Electricity Supply Bureau
	Broadcast and Television Bureau	Broadcast and Television Bureau
		Broadcast and Television Company
	Staff and Workers Education Office	Staff and Workers Education Office[1]
	Suzhou Television University	Suzhou Television University
	Salt Industry Company	Salt Industry Company
	Tobacco Specialty Sales Bureau	Tobacco Specialty Sales Bureau
		Tobacco Company
		Cigarettes, Sugar and Liquor Company
	Weather Station	Weather Bureau
	Insurance Company	Insurance Company
People's Bank of China	People's Bank of China	People's Bank of China
Agricultural Bank of China	Agricultural Bank of China	Agricultural Bank of China
	People's Construction Bank of China	People's Construction Bank of China
	Industrial and Commercial Bank	Industrial and Commercial Bank
		Bank of Communications

Note:

1. Interviewed

Sources: Several interviews; *Kunshan dianhua haobu 1996* (*Kunshan telephone directory 1996*). Kunshan: Post and Telecommunications Bureau; *Kunshan xianzhi* (1990) (*Kunshan County Gazetteer*). Shanghai: Shanghai People's Publishers, pp. 254–264, 514–517.

commercialization and marketization of government functions within the old state-run command economy structures. The most important of these companies became integral components of the various industrial and commercial bureaux and related exchange and distribution organizations under the Planning and Economic Commissions (see Table 1). These companies also provided a significant proportion of the financing for their respective administrative organizations, including supplementary bonuses for state employees and the full salaries of other bureaucrats not covered by state allocations. Other companies were created solely in order to increase extrabudgetary revenues for the benefit of their respective bureaux and/or their clients, engaging in activities largely unrelated to the administrative functions of local government.

Table 1 also illustrates the emergence of specialized organizations which were created to manage and promote exchange and distribution for the large number of enterprises which were not part of the planned economy. Agencies such as the Rural Industry Bureau, the Economic Cooperation Commission, and the Economic and Technical Cooperation Office facilitated access to the means of production, technical and management expertise, and markets necessary for the successful development of local industrial enterprises. The nature of these linkages, interactions and interrelationships, and the institutional parameters which embodied them, are discussed in more detail below. Suffice it to say at this point that the emergence of these organizations, and their affiliated corporate-like entities, reflected dramatic changes in the local space economy.

At the town and village levels, overlap of civil administration, CCP affairs, and management of the economy was very apparent. Town and village CCP secretaries often served in government bureaux and frequently held directorships in the town's Economic Commission or related companies. Criteria used to assess the performance of these local cadres and, therefore, their level of remuneration, have become increasingly linked to the success of local economic development and the welfare of local residents.[11] Combined with fiscal pressures to increase the revenue base and to raise extrabudgetary funds for local economic development and social welfare, it was easy to see why town and village governments in Kunshan vigorously encouraged the expansion of rural non-agricultural activities.

Ownership and management of enterprises

In practice, the precise functioning of community level governments depended largely upon their ability to generate extrabudgetary revenues. In Kunshan, collectively owned town and village industrial enterprises became the most important source of such revenues. Thus, economic power and management authority in Kunshan were manifest through the operation of collectively owned community enterprises concentrated at the town and village levels. Under the supervision of the Kunshan Rural Industry Bureau, every town established an industrial corporation to oversee the operations of all town and village run industrial enterprises. In addition to its supervisory role, the Rural Industry Bureau provided a range of business services to the town industrial corporations and directly to rural enterprises. The Bureau also regulated and approved the development of enterprises and often acted on their behalf to seek the necessary permission from other parts of the Kunshan administration, such as the Land Management and Environmental Protection Bureaux, for the construction of factories in the countryside. More importantly, the Rural Industry Bureau would facilitate investment and exchange relationships, technological and management

---

[11] Ho, S. P. S. (1994) *Rural China in Transition: Non-agricultural Development in Rural Jiangsu, 1978–1990*. Oxford: Clarendon; Shue, V. (1988) *The Reach of the State: Sketches of the Chinese Body Politic*. Stanford: Stanford University Press.

cooperation, and the training of workers and managers. Another more specific mandate of the Bureau was to promote the development of rural industries that were linked directly to the agricultural sector and which would benefit local farmers. The Bureau itself had 39 employees, only 12 of whom were funded through state allocations. The bulk of the administration, including the 27 non-state employees, was funded through consulting fees collected from rural industrial enterprises and industrial corporations, and the revenues generated by 6 enterprises owned by the Bureau.

Town industrial corporations acted primarily as the branch of town governments that actually owned and operated town enterprises. These corporations, which also existed in many villages, functioned like holding companies with a board of directors who determined enterprise activities in consultation with managers and town governments. Town and village governments, for example, selected directors for their industrial corporations who would then appoint factory managers. There was, of course, much overlap of responsibility in these respective positions since local government officials frequently served as directors or deputy heads in the Industrial Corporations, and were sometimes intimately involved in the day to day operations of specific enterprises. As long as these enterprises made money, however, managers and the section heads they appointed usually operated with minimal interference from local governments. Similar to the Kunshan Rural Industry Bureau, industrial corporations also fulfilled other roles relating to the provision of certain services. These included market research for villages that intended to establish an enterprise, advice on the design and implementation of accounting systems, and the allocation and training of workers and management personnel. Similar to an industrial association, the corporation provided "member" enterprises access to services and expertise for a fee.

Through their supply and sales organizations the industrial corporations also negotiated access to inputs and markets for local enterprises. With the authority, representation, political connections, and entrepreneurial savvy of the town government supporting them, industrial corporations in Kunshan facilitated linkages between local enterprises and factory managers, emerging markets, the agricultural sector and, most importantly, the partially reformed command economy structures. In this context even the names of towns became important since the industrial corporations and many local enterprises bore the same name. Thus, the town of Chenmu in southern Kunshan, which means "old tomb" and is not an auspicious name for doing business, became Jinxi — "bright and beautiful brook" — in 1993. That same year, the town of Diandong ("East of Dian" [Lake]) became Dianshanhu ("Dianshan Lake") Town for the same reason (see Figure 2).[12] In addition to its economic functions, the town industrial corporation also provided "guidance" for the implementation of workplace safety regulations, labour standards including salaries, environmental protection rules, and supervised the finances and accounting practices of enterprises. Moreover, the industrial corporation had the power to force enterprise mergers or break-ups if circumstances were deemed appropriate.

Taken together, the administrative, regulatory, and economic functions of the town industrial corporations were said to provide the "internal engine of development".[13] Although town and some village governments had similar companies in the construction, commercial, and services sectors, in value terms they were less important than local industrial corporations. More about the precise transactional relationships and interactions will be discussed below, but it is clear at this point that such organizations embodied complex overlapping, apparently conflicting roles and responsibilities. The way in which

[12] Zhang, P. R. (1993) Diandong gong ming wei Dianshanhu zhen (Diandong changes name to Dianshanhu Town). *Kunshan jingji xinxi* (*Kunshan economic information*), April 20, p. 1.

[13] Interview notes.

these functions were negotiated and balanced reveals much about the underlying processes and mechanisms driving local development. Informants in Kunshan and other parts of the lower Yangzi delta repeatedly emphasized the importance of local industrial organizations and the way in which town and village governments "stimulated" and "encouraged" investment in local enterprises and the development of production and marketing linkages. These and other factors such as local restrictions on the growth of private industrial enterprises, served to reinforce the concentration of economic and administrative power, ownership, and management authority at the town and village levels and helps to explain the proliferation of industrial activities into all corners of the Kunshan countryside.

Spatial Proliferation of Enterprises

Since all town and village governments wished to develop their own enterprises as a source of extrabudgetary revenues this led to the scattering of factories across the countryside. While a number of these enterprises were located in or near the town seats, most were built among the rice paddies, wheat fields, and canola crops. The locational distribution of town and village enterprises was closely linked to the structure of ownership and the territorial extent of the respective administrative jurisdictions.[14] The most important group of enterprises in Kunshan included town and village level industries which together comprised 69.8 percent of the 2205 industrial enterprises and 58.5 percent of the gross value of industrial output in 1996. Town and

---

[14] See: Lee, Y. S. (1992) Rural transformation and decentralized urban growth in China. In Guldin, G. E. (Ed.) *Urbanizing China*. Westport: Greenwood, pp. 89–118; Tan, K. C. (1993) China's small town urbanization program: Criticism and rethinking. *Geojournal 29* (2), pp. 155–162, and; Zhang, Z. (1994) Development of rural township enterprises in China: Prospects and problems. *Biennial Conference of the Australian Asian Studies Association*. Perth, July 13–16.

village level enterprises included collectives (396), village factories (745), domestic joint ventures and cooperatives (252), and sino-foreign joint ventures (147) scattered throughout rural Kunshan. Most of the 132 wholly foreign owned industrial enterprises, which accounted for 31.0 percent of gross output value in 1996, were located in the Special Economic and Technological Development Zone just east of Yushan Town (see Figure 2). The 59 state enterprises were located in or near the built-up core of Kunshan or in the Red Flag Industrial Area (see Figure 2). Most of the 470 private enterprises were established in Kunshan's 466 villages. Kunshan had 4 joint stock enterprises in 1996. These figures do not include 997 small scale household based individual industrial enterprises which were listed separately in the official statistics.[15]

Linked to the desire of each administrative jurisdiction to maximize local productive opportunities, the sectoral structure of industry across towns and villages in Kunshan has also diversified. Moreover, the sectoral breakdown of industrial activities closely paralleled the distribution of such activities across the entire lower Yangzi delta region. Informants referred to numerous examples of how town and village governments, anxious to achieve the same success as neighbouring communities, invested in virtually identical activities.[16] In addition to the development of broadly similar industrial structures across the region, this spontaneous and haphazard growth created enormous problems related to the provision of infrastructure, duplication, and the waste of capital and land. With typical Chinese panache, allusions to such conditions were captured in a local slogan: *cun cun dianhuo, chu chu maoyan* (in every village fires stir, and

---

[15] (*KSTJNJ*) *Kunshan tongji nianjian 1996* (*Kunshan statistical yearbook 1996*). Kunshan: Kunshan Statistical Publishers, p. 115.
[16] Interview notes.

everywhere is belching smoke).[17] While such industrial development was "comprehensive" and relatively successful at the local scale, in regional terms (county level and higher) it remained "irrational" and spatially scattered.

In conceptual terms, the diverse structure and spatial proliferation of industrial activities in Kunshan strongly suggests that the rural transformation observed here occurred largely as a response to intensely localized development imperatives. The result was a dense mixture of residential, industrial, and agricultural land uses. Official concern with the loss of highly productive agricultural land has prompted the creation of specially designated agricultural protection zones in several towns in Kunshan and across the lower Yangzi delta. That such measures were necessary in one of China's richest farming regions says much about the proliferation of non-agricultural activities and hints at the inherent tensions and conflicts which underlie the spatial economic transformation occurring here. The means by which these issues were negotiated and resolved, and the institutional structures that emerged to control and manage the local economy are introduced in the next section.

Formalizing Local Institutional Structures in a Partially Reformed Command Economy

In addition to demonstrating the inadequacy of conventional approaches which emphasize the role of external economies in regional development, the findings presented thus far highlight the need to understand the way in which specific cultural, political, and historical circumstances led to the emergence of institutional structures which controlled and managed economic activity in Kunshan. As will be

---

[17] Qinghua University Urban-Rural Development Research Group (1995) Suxichang diqu chengxiang kongjian huanjing fazhan guihua yanjiu (Suxichang area urban-rural spatial environment development planning research). Beijing: Qinghua University.

demonstrated below, these localized structures embodied stratification by bureaucratic hierarchy rather than by market competition and opportunity. These realities in Kunshan should be distinguished from the social stratification and variations in the modes of production motifs advocated in the conventional wisdom.[18]

Capitalism with Chinese characteristics

What emerged during the pre-reform period as local strategies and sub-cultures of economic (and political) survival had blossomed by the late 1980s into a kind of bureaucratic capitalism whereby "socialist wheeler dealers" pertinaciously served local interests while enhancing their own power.[19] This power was manifest and exercised in several ways. The power and prestige of local cadres in Kunshan was based upon their capacity to negotiate their community's relationship and obligations to the centre. These interactions occurred through personal relations or *guanxi* and via intensely localized administrative and institutional structures that represented local interests. Kunshan was thus able to accumulate resources for its own development by engagement with, and manipulation of the partially reformed command economy structures. Kunshan and community level bureaucrats would reinterpret and distort the rules of the partially reformed planned economy structures and bend the guidelines of state managed finance to "make full use of the official policies in as flexible a way as possible" to benefit local development.[20] The

---

[18] See for example: Booth, D. (1993) Development Research: From Impasse to New Agenda. In Schuurman, F. J. (Ed.) *Beyond the Impasse: New Directions in Development Theory*. London: Zed, pp. 49-76, and; Huang, P. C. C. (1990) *The Peasant Family and Rural Development in the Yangzi Delta, 1350–1988*. Stanford: Stanford University Press.

[19] Shue, V. (1988) *op. cit.*

[20] Interview notes.

most common refrain heard in this regard was "above there is policy, below we have strategy" (*shang you zhengce, xia you jice*, or sometimes *duice* — "countermeasures"). One especially perceptive informant referred to *cabian qiu* — the phenomenon in Ping-Pong whereby a player attempts to direct the ball as close as possible to the opponent's edge of the table without going off.

The multiple roles and interests of local governments also meant that issues of enterprise scale and location were often decided administratively for what might otherwise be seen as marginal investments.[21] Numerous officials interviewed throughout the lower Yangzi delta, as well as in Kunshan, spoke passionately about local initiatives, particularly with respect to major infrastructural investments, despite obvious duplication or disarticulation with similar endeavours in neighbouring jurisdictions. When pressed to explain how such investments were considered economically viable, local officials referred to specific means by which they could guarantee the success of such initiatives. These included administrative decrees that forced enterprises within their jurisdiction to purchase locally produced goods, to utilize local services or infrastructure, and the implementation of various administrative barriers to "protect" these local investments from outside competition.

The spatial economic implications of such intense localism were reflected in the emergence of what some have termed "palace economies", in which economic efficiencies were subordinated by administrative imperatives linked to areas of jurisdiction, authority, and power.[22] Taken together, these factors contributed to the downward

[21] Watson, A. (1992) The management of the rural economy: The institutional parameters. In Watson, A. (Ed.) *Economic reform and social change in China*. New York: Routledge, pp. 171–199.

[22] Watson, A. (1992) *op. cit.*; Wu, H. X. (Wu, H. X. Y.) (1994) Rural enterprise contributions to growth and structural change. In Findlay, C., Watson, A. & Wu, H. X. (Eds.) *Rural enterprises in China*. New York: St. Martin's, pp. 39–68.

dispersion of economic power away from the centre. Clearly, this trend was also prone to deep distortion and corruption within conditions elsewhere labeled "capitalism with Chinese characteristics".[23] As a result, Kunshan was able to manage its economy as a discrete, autonomous entity and to strongly influence the way in which it related to the regional, national, and global economies.

Individual interactions and interrelationships

The success of community development largely depended upon the expertise, experience, and entrepreneurial savvy of local cadres, workers, and other individuals. The management and technical skills that had built up in Kunshan over the years was thus drawn upon to support the development of local enterprises. Such expertise sometimes came from local residents who had been sent earlier to work in cities, but who were returned to the countryside in the 1960s and 1970s. In addition to their particular skills and experience, they also brought social connections and networks that would become important later in terms of obtaining market information and other assistance. Informants in Kunshan also referred to another group of individuals, who emerged from the political campaigns of the Cultural Revolution, who played an important role in local development. Between 1968 and 1976 more than a million Shanghai youths were rusticated to remote parts of China.[24] Although some have since been permitted to return to Shanghai most were not, so many of them chose to settle in places nearby such as Kunshan. The establishment of numerous successful local enterprises was directly associated with these individuals and their families who provided links not only with Shanghai, but also with the region and

---

[23] Marton, A. M. (1994) Challenges for metrofitting the lower Yangtze delta. *Western geography 4*, pp. 62–83

[24] *Shanghai jingji 1949–1982* (*Shanghai economy 1949-1982*). Shanghai: Shanghai Academy of Social Sciences.

units to which they had been sent earlier. One of many notable examples was a group of several dozen Shanghai natives returned from Chengdu in Sichuan Province who set up a factory in Chengbei Town to manufacture watch components. Between 1987 and 1989 the Kunshan government even had an office in the capital of Guizhou Province in southwest China that facilitated such arrangements.[25]

It also became clear early on in the fieldwork that several prominent officials in Kunshan were formerly high ranking People's Liberation Army commanders who had been transferred by choice to key civilian posts (*zhuanye*). One such individual who was recognized for his superb administrative and entrepreneurial skills in the military arrived in Kunshan in 1988 and was, by 1991, a vice-director of the Municipal Civil Affairs Bureau. Promoted by 1993 to the directorships of the Kunshan Economic System Reform Commission and the Economic Research Centre, he was also deeply involved in a number of local development activities including promoting Kunshan as part of a trade and investment delegation in his former military region in China's northeast.

Enterprises in Kunshan also took advantage of every available opportunity to establish linkages with technical and management expertise from outside the region. Senior and retired cadres from enterprises and bureaux in Shanghai, for example, were hired on a contract basis to provide advice, expertise, and were sometimes invited to invest in local enterprises. Famous for its fishing, Kunshan attracted many older Shanghai experts who were recruited quite literally while casting from the banks of local waterways. Supplementing meagre pensions from state enterprises with attractive benefits, many lived in Kunshan to run factories full-time, or commuted regularly as "weekend engineers" (*zhoumo gongchengshi*).[26] Other economic

---

25 Interview notes.
26 Interview notes.

interactions emerged largely from personal connections and other social relationships.

Coinciding with a critical change of leadership in 1984, the Kunshan government began encouraging enterprises and individuals to find ways of establishing linkages outside the region. By 1985 the county government had established a special office under the auspices of the new Economic Cooperation Commission to promote technical, management, investment, and production and marketing cooperation (see Table 1). While Shanghai, and later the new zone in Pudong across from downtown Shanghai, were the main focus of such endeavours, by 1992 the Kunshan government also had representative offices in Nanjing, Beijing, and Shenzhen which facilitated local linkages. In addition, there were hundreds of other town, village, enterprise, and individual agents and representatives located throughout China. A key element of the reform changes in Kunshan highlighted by local informants was this "opening-up" to the outside and a fundamental shift in outlook initiated by the new mayor in 1984. While the imperatives and outcomes of community development in Kunshan remained intensely localized, many had come to recognize the value of external linkages and cooperation. By the early 1990s, the Kunshan level bureaucracy and town and village governments had established institutional structures to promote, control, and manage this increasingly interactive transactional environment.

Horizontal and vertical linkages

Transactional linkages, and other economic interrelationships relevant for local economic development in Kunshan, were cultivated along two sometimes intersecting streams (*shuang gui, shuang cheng* — literally "double tracks, double levels"). The first included horizontal linkages (*hengxiang lianxi*) arising largely from the kind of relationships described above. Seen more as commercially based arrangements that crossed regions and administrative boundaries, these linkages also tended to eschew bureaucratic hierarchies taking advantage of opportunities to "capture" talent, capital, information, and markets within and outside Kunshan. While often pursued and promoted through local government institutional structures, the development of such linkages relied less on the functional relationships of government bureaucracies than on the connections between individuals, enterprises, and local collective entities.

The second type of interaction cultivated by the local government was referred to as vertical linkages (*zhongxiang lianxi*). These linkages followed the bureaucratic and administrative hierarchy more closely than did horizontal linkages. While they were also frequently based on personal connections and guanxi, the resulting transactional relationships relied on negotiated access to, and sometimes subversion of, the partially reformed command economy structures. It is clear from Table 1 that a large number of institutional structures emerged in Kunshan to manage and manipulate these linkages. Those concerned with specific industrial sectors, for example, were hived off from the local Economic Commission in the early 1990s.

The Kunshan Machinery, Electronics and Metallurgical Industries Bureau, and the Textiles Bureau were both established in 1991 to strengthen linkages with the respective provincial and prefectural level bureaux responsible for these sectors (see Table 1). Most of the benefits for local enterprises were of a commercial nature, including assured and subsidized access to raw materials, energy, skilled labour, and increased access to stable sales channels in the state sector. In addition to their regulatory functions, and the provision of professional, technical, and management services (for a fee), these bureaux also allowed Kunshan authorities to play a greater role in provincial and prefectural level decisions regarding planning and policy and, most importantly, to lobby for preferential treatment. In close collaboration with the Economic Cooperation Commission, discussed below, these bureaux established and cultivated the horizontal linkages described above, while their corporate branches executed the commercial transactions directly on behalf of Kunshan level enterprises or, via the Rural Industry Bureau, for town and village collectives.

Entirely locally financed, these Kunshan based institutional structures emerged to provide a link between local development interests and the hierarchies of the partially reformed command economy structures. It is noteworthy, perhaps even ironic, that the rapid development of rural enterprises in Kunshan outside the command economy was fueled in part by an equally rapid expansion in the power and intervention of local government. Of course, the local bureaucracy was profoundly more responsive and flexible than the former planned economy structures as it was able to pursue and cultivate opportunities quickly and independently for the benefit of local enterprises. Despite official policies which attempted to separate government administration and the economy, it is clear that the emergence of various institutional structures in Kunshan in fact strengthened and exploited this relationship. The nature of this relationship is explored further in the following section.

The Economic Cooperation Commission

Perhaps the most interesting of the bureaucratic arrangements devised to encourage and manage these horizontal and vertical linkages, and the resulting transactional activities, was the Kunshan Economic Cooperation Commission (ECC) mentioned above and in Table 1. By the mid-1980s local governments in Kunshan realized that rapid industrial growth would not continue unless town and village enterprises could gain more stable access to inputs, markets, investment, and technological and management expertise. While enterprises technically had the freedom to arrange commercial and other linkages, usually through local level purchasing and sales companies, acting on their own they often confronted obstacles. With the opening up of markets the sales of output were generally less problematic than the procurement of inputs. As one informant explained,

> "... town and village enterprises were not part of the state plan so there was always trouble with purchasing materials ... town and village governments did not have adequate access to resources of their own, nor did they have the necessary connections for trade ... information was difficult to obtain and they didn't know where to go for supplies and skilled people".[27]

Thus, in 1984 Kunshan responded to these concerns by establishing the ECC with the goal of providing a conduit to the means of production and sales opportunities for the increasing number of town and village enterprises. Through town offices of the ECC, local enterprises became linked to a complex set of networks and transactional relationships coordinated by "agents" in the Kunshan level bureaucracy. Most personnel in the ECC had previously worked in local branches of the command economy system such as the Goods and Materials Bureau or the Supply and Sales Office (see Table 1). Other employees included representatives from the Kunshan Planning and Economic Commissions who were interested in obtaining information about procurement and sales opportunities for state run and Kunshan level enterprises in order to supplement their planned quotas. Not only were these individuals familiar with the circumstances of local industrial development, they also had intimate knowledge of and connections within the hierarchies of the planned economy.

The specific tasks of the ECC included facilitating the exchange of materials by organizing special transactions, and the brokering of economic and technological cooperation between town and village enterprises in Kunshan and enterprises and other organizations outside

---

[27] Interview notes.

Kunshan. The dealmaking coordinated by the ECC was innovative and wide ranging. While many of the linkages and contacts were still based upon networks of personal relations, through family, friends, and business or bureau associates, the resulting transactional arrangements had become quite sophisticated. Before the early 1980s, for example, a typical transaction might have involved a state run factory in Shanghai supplying old equipment to a town or village enterprise in exchange for agricultural products. These one-time barter agreements still occurred and usually involved Kunshan providing quantities of rice or edible oil for coal and other materials. However, with the establishment of the ECC in 1984, transactional relationships became more complicated, sometimes involving different types of investment including the sale of local enterprises to outside interests. While the ECC might coordinate investments, or other joint technological or management arrangements, most enterprises remained locally owned and operated, even as they acquired a more flexible and open attitude based on these experiences.

The ECC also cultivated critically important transactional arrangements across hierarchies of the planned economy. These relationships did not follow the conventional vertical patterns of interaction as in the state plan. Rather, they tended to intersect where opportunities arose, usually among enterprises at a similar levels of the command economy hierarchy, and cutting across the administrative and geographical boundaries, or bureaucratic space, that delineated the flow of goods and materials. In 1992 for example, the ECC brokered access to a stable supply of coal for local enterprises, including a small power station in Qiandeng Town, by arranging a reciprocal investment scheme. Certain local governments and particular enterprises invested more than RMB 10 million in coal production and related facilities in Shaanxi Province, while the local branch of the coal supply bureau in Shaanxi invested in the power station in Qiandeng. Prior to this the power station lost money and the Kunshan enterprises involved experienced difficulties because of the insecure and more expensive supply of coal available outside the state plan. Under the new arrangement, Kunshan gained a stable supply of subsidized coal for local enterprises while the relevant bureau in Shaanxi supplemented its income with an agreed upon proportion of the earnings from the now profitable power station.[28]

Perhaps the most fascinating transactional relations brokered by the ECC involved the exchange of quotas or allocations (*zhi biao*). Although there was usually no direct documented exchange of quotas or allocations *per se*, as with state controlled procurement and sales of key commodities and the transfer of printed ration coupons for example, transactions were negotiated as if there were. As one informant explained, "local quotas utilized in such transactions had to be replaced with quotas of other things". For example, the ECC might arrange for the relevant bureau to sell a portion of Kunshan's state allocation of subsidized rice to another region in exchange for the opportunity for local enterprises to purchase required inputs. More often, however, the ECC would arrange for town and village enterprises to sell popular consumer goods or industrial products to enterprises and bureaux outside Kunshan in order to secure inputs or sales opportunities for other local enterprises. Coordinating particular exchanges, and helping to establish other linkages between enterprises, was also facilitated by providing relevant information regarding available resources and markets.

As has been alluded to throughout this section, the ECC and other local institutional structures also wielded enormous influence over town and village enterprises. These agencies were able to ensure that the activities of local enterprises were compatible with the objectives of the Kunshan government by controlling and manipulating access to preferential transactional relationships, loans and other sources of

---

[28]   Interview notes.

capital, tax concessions and subsidies, and other administratively determined commercial advantages. Chinese companies from outside Kunshan who were interested in establishing an enterprise here, most often approached the ECC to identify potential partners, to help arrange local joint ventures. The power and authority of the ECC in facilitating such linkages was utilized to induce the compliance of local enterprises and even local governments. This influence also extended to the large number of enterprises who had managers and technical experts from outside Kunshan. These individuals were invited by the ECC at least twice a year to a working meeting to openly discuss their experiences in Kunshan and to explore ways in which certain problems could be "solved".

County level agencies with functions similar to the ECC existed in most advanced regions throughout China, so there was ample scope to facilitate the transactions necessary to support local industrial development in Kunshan. In addition to the increased opportunities for production and sales stimulated by market-like economic reforms, therefore, the ECC and other local institutional structures coordinated access to more stable and subsidized supplies of inputs and to "assured" or "contracted" markets for town and village enterprises. Informants reported in 1992 that about one-quarter of the industrial enterprises in Kunshan (excluding individual enterprises) had initiated ongoing cooperative linkages of some kind with units outside Kunshan. To emphasize the importance of such linkages, these enterprises were responsible for nearly two-thirds of the gross value of industrial output and nearly three-quarters of net earnings from industry in Kunshan, according to local officials. Most of these enterprises were scattered across the Kunshan countryside, leading the transformation of the rural economy.

This section has provided insights into the processes and mechanisms whereby rural communities in Kunshan constructed industrial space by utilizing certain forms of representation. The emergence of particular local administrative and institutional parameters were a central element of regional spatial economic transformation in the lower Yangzi delta. These institutional structures embodied a complex web of interactions and interrelationships tied to particular places. Kunshan, town and village level cadres, who exercised powerful influence through these intensely localized structures, managed and manipulated the transactional networks, frequently creating new ones, in order to maximize community based productive opportunities. This helps to explain the diffuse nature of rural industrial development in Kunshan. Also obvious from this analysis was the paradox of local institutional structures, which sought to manipulate and overcome the administrative boundaries and bureaucratic space of the partially reformed command economy, while at the same time constructing their own protected space for local industrial development.

Moreover, by taking advantage of their position to influence crucial linkages in the transactional environment, community governments strengthened their role in local development in Kunshan, rather than separating from the economy as they were obliged according to official policy. This was possible, in part, because conventional market mechanisms, such as factor mobility and real prices that would truly reflect cost and scarcity, did not prevail in the Chinese economy.[29] In fact, the intersection of new market-like opportunities and incentives that arose from the reform measures initiated in the late 1970s, and the monolithic structures of the planned economy, were manifested in Kunshan by the emergence of administrative and institutional structures which have assumed many of the features of the old system rather than changing it. While the result has been a flourishing of interactions and interrelationships, the concomitant downward dispersion of economic and administrative power has deepened the parochialism and

[29]   Fan, C. C. (1995) Of belts and ladders: State policy and uneven regional development in post-Mao China. *Annals of the association of American geographers 85* (3), pp. 421–449.

balkanization of localities, even as it has empowered them to develop economic linkages with other regions and to determine, and sometimes redefine, the way in which local industrial concerns conducted their exchange relations and other transactional activities.

Repositioning Locality

This paper has highlighted a number of issues which need to be accommodated in a new conceptual framework for understanding rural-urban transformation in the lower Yangzi delta and the geography of enterprise location in particular. The common theme to emerge is the way in which rural enterprises were linked, through dense networks of highly localized physical and administrative infrastructure, to a wide array of other places and institutional structures, both within and outside Kunshan. These elements were linked together in their mutual constitution as part of the transactional environment.

The transactional environment encompassed "standard" (economic) largely measurable transactional activities and less obvious, but ultimately more important, individual and institutional relationships and interdependencies, which mediated these activities, as manifested and articulated through various transactional networks. The creation of new transactional networks, and the recapturing and modification of former networks, led to the emergence of intensely localized administrative and institutional structures which managed and were in turn influenced by the processes and mechanisms of spatial economic transformation in Kunshan. It was these transactional networks, moreover, which played a fundamental role in determining the production of industrial space in Kunshan and which also provide the key to understanding what it is that determines the unique patterns and processes of rural-urban transformation in China.

What then are the implications of this case study of Kunshan for conceptualizing the underlying processes in other mega-urban regions in China? While the particular features of development in Kunshan and the lower Yangzi delta may not be duplicated elsewhere, the analysis here strongly suggests that specific local circumstances need to be carefully considered for a greater appreciation of the full complexity of rural-urban transition. Moreover, while linkages with large city cores were clearly important in such regions, it was the emergence of a spatially dispersed, but highly integrated and dense transactional environment which contributed to the in situ stabilization or resilience of local production systems. Deeply rooted in locality and place, it was this transactional environment and its largely self-generated transactions of growth which propelled spatial economic restructuring in the Kunshan countryside. Furthermore, these rapidly restructuring regions, with a previously distant presence in the hierarchy of non-agricultural production systems (at least during the more recent collectivist past), have by many measures equaled or exceeded long established industrial centres. Can the Kunshan countryside continue to be considered "rural"? Is all or part of Kunshan "urban"? In the context of the approach advocated here, these distinctions are less important than understanding the processes and mechanisms which have affected the emergence of such highly productive mixed agricultural and non-agricultural regions.

This approach must also capture the paradox of economic development as it was linked to the expanding power and influence of local governments to promote growth, and the rising appreciation of, and localized attempts to respond to, external economies and the dynamics of conventional agglomeration. Yet the evidence strongly suggests that the intensely localized processes and mechanisms driving regional economic restructuring in the lower Yangzi delta will persist for some time. While the resulting patterns of agricultural and non-agricultural development will likely deepen, their fundamental character will remain essentially unchanged. It is possible to make this assertion with some certainty since intensely localized and deeply embedded place-based features of this restructuring which will not easily change under the current circumstances.

On the other hand, is there a point in the regional transformation at which agglomerative tendencies will take over? Is the spatial economic restructuring observed in the lower Yangzi delta merely a transitional phase preceding the growth of large more concentrated urban agglomerations? Such developments would need to include changes to or elimination of the influence of administrative and institutional structures which have profoundly mediated the local geography of enterprises. This might involve the revamping of ownership and property rights to allow for free market transfers of land and capital, meaningful tax measures to redistribute the benefits of economic development, or banking and financial reforms which entrenched commercial, rather than politically motivated decision making. Such changes imply the decoupling of administrative and institutional parameters from locality and place which might adversely affect the underlying processes and mechanisms driving economic development in the first place. A similar outcome might also emerge in any case as a consequence of severe environmental degradation and the haphazard consumption of arable land by non-agricultural development.

Conventional processes and patterns of urbanization may also occur as a result of the strengthening of external economies and enhancing the dynamics of agglomeration through further economic reforms. The nature of the product structure and the distribution of external markets becomes important in this context. Will endogenous factors in Kunshan continue to dominate the character of local development if there was a shift in the type of commodities it produced and to whom they were sold? If Kunshan were, for example, to increase exports of consumer products to Shanghai or foreign markets, issues such as efficiency and quality, technology and capital inputs, and product cycles might be expected to exercise greater influence over key interactions and inter-relationships which determine the local geography of production.

Increased access and exposure to the global economy including, among other things, a freer domestic marketplace that reflected true prices, would more directly affect the transactional and production activities of enterprises, perhaps stimulating greater economies of scale and other efficiencies. Adjustments in the structure of ownership and management that this implies would entail a fundamental shift in the relationship between local governments and enterprises. While there is some recent evidence to suggest that such a shift is underway, without commensurate adjustments elsewhere in the system, such changes might stimulate even greater administrative interference to protect and promote local enterprises.[30]

Whatever the possible scenarios, the preceding case study of Kunshan demonstrates that conceptualizing urban transformation in China must necessarily highlight the complex interactions and interrelationships underlying spatial economic restructuring. The specific implications of a conceptual and analytical emphasis on local circumstances for policy formation and strategic planning are introduced in the final section of this paper.

Planning and Management Agenda:
Chinese Solutions for Chinese Problems

This study has highlighted a fundamental reorientation towards the critical dimensions of locality and place as they have determined the character of local and regional change in the lower Yangzi delta. However, the critical dimensions of spatial economic restructuring in the delta., while largely rooted and defined by locality and place, were not confined to small scale disaggregated units. Confronting the challenges for planning and management of the lower Yangzi delta

---

[30] Interview notes.

region requires that these dimensions are perceived not just in terms of their particularities, but also in terms of their conjectural nature and articulation across the wider space economy. Therefore, this section will introduce three broad sets of priorities which frame an agenda for the planning and management of the lower Yangzi delta which responds to this approach. The first revolves around issues of spatial relations between varying socio-economic fields. The term 'socio-economic field' is introduced here to refer to regions, spatially and conceptually, between urban and rural, and which are difficult to clearly define as either. The second addresses administrative and institutional structures which influence decision making and control. The third set of priorities is concerned with information needs, data gathering, and monitoring.

If regional transformation is reconceptualized as a function of interactions and interrelationships over space, the formation of planning policies must also recognize and respond to the specificities of intensely localized processes and mechanisms which underlie these linkages and their constituent transactional networks. The functional relationships among the many actors within and between socio-economic fields in the lower Yangzi delta were more complex, for example, than merely the general extension of urban influence over the hinterland. Yet the assumptions implicit in most responses to the spatial economic restructuring in such regions underlines how economic actors in large cites were seen to provide the impetus for change, or how transformation in the countryside was supposedly determined by proximity to urban metropolis. Growth profiles and development scenarios based on these assumptions frequently envisage industrial relocation from urban core into the surrounding countryside, and the filling-up of rural areas which previously contained only insignificant levels of non-agricultural activity.[31]

---

[31] Chreod Ltd. (1996) The Yangzi delta megalopolis. *International Conference on Towards a Sustainable Future*, Qinghua University, Beijing, April 26, pp. 4, 6–10.

The resulting planning and management agendas ignored or overlooked critical underlying elements of spatial economic transformation in the lower Yangzi delta. The importance and persistence of highly productive farming, especially of staple food commodities, and its juxtaposition with the growth and proliferation of non-agricultural activities was a common example. Calls for the development of transportation including arterial routes between major centres, the exploitation of existing networks, and increased flexibility in transportation modes were another example.[32] Noble and necessary objectives, they were reflected in the recently completed Shanghai-Nanjing Expressway and other bridge, highway, railway, and port development projects. However, by focusing on these high profile and costly mega-projects, attention was drawn away from critically important local level practical realities. Regional integration and planning of transport infrastructure in the delta were, for example in constant conflict with the objectives of community governments who spoke passionately about local initiatives, but generally lacked a broader regional perspective.

Therefore, planning and management strategies in the lower Yangzi delta must hinge upon issues at once broader and more specific than those most frequently emphasized. This requires a fundamental reorientation of the way in which such regions are conceptualized. Several Chinese studies have attempted to provide a conceptual and analytical middle ground by invoking notions of rural-urban symbiosis (*chengxiang yitihua*) or "unity" (*xietiao chengxiang guanxi*).[33] While

---

[32] *Ibid.*, p. 4; McGee, T. G. (1995) Metrofitting the Emerging Mega-Urban Regions of ASEAN: An Overview. In McGee, T. G. & Robinson, I. M. (Eds.), The Mega-Urban Regions of Southeast Asia. Vancouver: UBC press, pp. 16–20.

[33] Duan, X. M. (1993) Nongcun gaige he fazhan mianlin de xin wenti (Facing the new problems of rural reform and development) *Zhongguo nongcun jingji* (*Chinese Rural Economy*) (8), p. 19; Zhang, L. J. (1989) *Chengxiang yitihua zhilu* (*The path of urban-rural symbiosis*) Beijing: Rural Reading Materials Press; Zhang, Y. L.

much of this work refers to the conventional distinction between "urban" and "rural", it also refocused attention on the interactions and interrelationships which link various socio-economic fields as they construct revitalized intervening regions of economic activity. Some Chinese planners have responded by generating development scenarios which emphasize the (re-)emergence of such regions and their important morphological characteristics. Referred to as "clustered mixed-use ecological communities" (*zutuan shiduoyong shengtai shequ*) this perspective evokes the processes and mechanisms highlighted in the preceding analysis.[34]

Implications for the planning and management agenda for the lower Yangzi delta are manifest. Many local and regional development practitioners in China were deeply critical of official policies embedded in the slogans "leave the land, but not the countryside; enter the factory, but not the city" (*litu, bulixiang; jinchang, bujincheng*) which tended to obscure the need to create well planned integrated regions by breaking down rural-urban, interregional, and local barriers. The steady development of agriculture could be ensured, for example, only through the continuous "restructuring" of "business circles" in the countryside by allowing peasants to "leave the land in order to leave the countryside" (*litu yilixiang*) and to "enter the factory and enter the city" (*jinchang youjincheng*).[35] This would help reduce the tension between competing land-uses in a more "unified" spatial structure of agriculture and

(1989) Woguo chengxiang guanxi de lishi kaocha (Historical overview of urban-rural relations in China). *Zhongguo nongcun jingji* (*Chinese Rural Economy*) (10), p. 8 (second part of a study which appeared in two issues).

[34] Qinghua University Urban-Rural Development Research Group (1995) *op. cit.*, pp. 57–58.

[35] See: Zhang S. C. (1991) Fazhan zhongxinzhen de jidian kanfa (Several views on developing central towns). *Jiangsu mingzheng* (*Jiangsu civil administration*) (24), p. 41; Zhang, S. C. (1996) *Kunshan fazhan guiji jishi* (*A record of Kunshan's course of development*). Nanjing: Jiangsu People's Press; and several interviews with the above author.

industry. The basic element of this approach would involve the development of central towns "positioned" in such a way as to "gather the functions" of the regional economy. This would include serving as the "global company" (*huanqiu gongsi*) for exchange relationships, as centres of culture and social welfare, capital, technology and information, and the markets for labour.

The underlying objective would not be recentralization or large scale urbanization, but rather to promote the integration of a restructuring countryside with big cities by strengthening the functions of appropriately positioned smaller central towns. This necessarily includes the development and improvement of tertiary services to enhance the circulation of capital, technology, information, and labour, and the efficient exchange of goods to encourage enterprises to relocate from the periphery to the vicinity of town seats. Establishing well serviced and appropriately situated special development zones in some towns, and at the county level, would help to stimulate more coordinated, less haphazard land uses. Such strategies also conform to the contours of the pre-modern period during which vibrant economic exchange between rural and urban sectors was channeled through small market towns and larger county level towns.

Some have envisaged similar planning objectives which sought to manage the regional transformation in other parts of Asia by developing smaller centres.[36] However, the resulting implementation strategies which emerged from these plans focused on the need for institutional changes which included increasing decentralization of decision making

---

[36] Douglass, M. (1995) Global interdependence and urbanization: Planning for the Bangkok mega-urban region. In McGee, T. G. & Robinson, I. M. (Eds.) *op. cit.*, pp. 71–74; Douglass. M. (1998) A regional network strategy for reciprocal rural-urban linkages: An agenda for policy research with reference to Indonesia. Third world planning review 20 (1), pp. 1–33; Robinson, I. M. (1995) Emerging spatial patterns in ASEAN mega-urban regions: Alternative strategies. In McGee, T. G. & Robinson, I. M. (Eds.) *op. cit.*, pp. 78–79, 85.

and control. Circumstances in the lower Yangzi delta suggest, on the other hand, the need for a more coordinated set of policies which coopt, or at least accommodate, exceedingly powerful and divergent local interests into a more meaningful regional plan. Planning is one thing, as it turns out, and implementation quite another. Or as one key informant remarked whimsically, "planning is rich, but development is poor" (*fu guihua, qiong kaifa*). This brings us to the second set of priorities which help shape the planning and management agenda for the delta.

Perhaps the greatest challenge for planning and policy formation in the lower Yangzi delta region relates to issues of management, decision making and control. Once again a fundamental reorientation of perspective is required. For example, the key findings of this study contradict the suggestion that the forces which have stimulated spatial economic restructuring in such regions transcended political boundaries, administrative areas, and ideology.[37] In fact, the problem facing planners is the way in which territorially based local administrations are able to manage their economies as discrete, autonomous entities. The prominent role of community governments in this context was to utilize administrative rather than economic means to vigorously promote their own interests against regional or national interests. While the reforms have stimulated new exigencies and opportunities within an increasingly intense transactional environment, this has not been matched by the commensurate development of appropriate administrative and regulatory structures. The planning and management agenda for the delta needs to include administrative and institutional changes that would encourage the development of more open transactional relationships across administrative boundaries. This can only occur by

---

[37] Ginsburg, N (1991) Preface. In Ginsburg, N. Koppel, B. & McGee, T. G. (Eds.) *The Extended Metropolis: Settlement Transition in Asia*. Honolulu: University of Hawaii Press, p. xvii.

introducing mechanisms to ensure that local governments see their role as providing incentives, efficient services, and an appropriate regulatory environment, to develop production rationally and in a sustainable manner, rather than "bolstering" their own socio-economic and political power through bureaucratic intervention.[38]

While there are some limited *ad hoc* efforts to tackle this problem through reforming ownership structures and the implementation of a transparent system of property rights, local governments retain tight, though perhaps increasingly less direct, influence over local enterprises. Reducing the interference of local governments in the economy could also occur through the restructuring and adjustment of administrative boundaries and the authority of local governments.[39] These changes must confront particular phenomena such as the centrifugal tendencies of local governments which pull economic power away from established centres. Contrary to those who have suggested that the "centrality" of an "urban place" in China is strengthened following reclassification to higher administrative status, the evidence from Kunshan has demonstrated how such administrative changes were rather more complex.[40] After Kunshan's elevation to "city" status, all of its 20 townships also achieved greater administrative and economic power by reclassification as designated towns. Perhaps the strengthening of county level administrations does not have to result in a commensurate upgrading of lower level bureaucracies.

---

[38] Watson, A. (1992) *op. cit.*, p. 182.

[39] Currently, Chinese research into such administrative divisions reforms remains highly sensitive. However, for an excellent summary of recent studies which review some of the relevant issues see: Liu. J. D. (1996) (Ed.) *Zhongguo xingzheng quhua de lilun yu shijian* (*Chinese administrative divisions: Theory and practice*). Shanghai: East China Normal University Press.

[40] Tan, K. C. (1993) China's small town urbanization program: Criticism and rethinking. *Geojournal 29* (2), p. 161.

Another approach to institutional reform would focus specifically on the need for some sort of administrative authority at the regional (lower Yangzi delta) scale, perhaps including sectoral sub-components. Theses might function initially as business organizations within government bureaux to coordinate and plan across the entire region. Objectives would include balancing and redistributing earnings as necessary, the introduction of more unhindered competition to encourage local comparative advantages, and mechanisms to prevent duplication and waste.[41] These objectives would not be realized in the case of the lower Yangzi delta through increased decentralization of decision making and control as some have proposed for other regions in Asia.[42] Instead, the priorities for administrative and institutional changes should include increasing the participation of local authorities in regional level decision making. The regional administrative and institutional amalgamation this suggests could be achieved through the creation of new alliances and networks. Through a kind of "opportunistic local incrementalism" these networks would be negotiated and balanced, for the benefit of regional planning and management of the delta, based on various financial and socio-political incentives.[43]

There is, of course, historical precedent in the lower Yangzi delta for the grassroots coordination of community level action for regional benefit. Enlightened local officials during late imperial times, occasionally with the encouragement and support of the state, drew

[41] Liu, J. D. *et al.* (1992) Rationalizing coastal development: A proposal to coordinate planning and management of Shanghai ports. International conference on urban land use and transport systems, Shanghai, June 8–12.
[42] McGee, T. G. & Robinson, I. M. (1995) ASEAN mega-urbanization: A synthesis. In McGee, T. G. & Robinson, I. M. (Eds.) *op. cit.* p. 354.
[43] The term is borrowed from R. J. R. Kirkby as he used it during the *Workshop on Reinterpreting Contemporary Urban Development Theory on Mega-Urban Regions in the Asia Pacific Context.* (1995) Vancouver, December 13–15.

upon pre-existing community organizations to respond to the issues of water control and management across large parts of the delta.[44] As in the past, however, implementing the administrative and institutional changes necessary to address contemporary planning and management challenges in the delta requires bridging the deep divisions of local interests and power.

Finally, the planning and management agenda for the lower Yangzi delta must also address the issues of information needs, data gathering, and monitoring. The intensity of the transactional environment, multiplicity of apparently incompatible land uses, and concerns about environmental degradation require the development of new systems of monitoring, data collection, and dissemination. Data collection in China generally occurs regularly, rapidly, and at a small enough scale to help identify areas of change. The problems are with accuracy and availability of these data. Although the accuracy and dissemination of official statistics has improved, there is a need to reexamine the framework within which it occurs. Data gathering necessarily relies upon a highly decentralized system of reporting, but which is subject to the vested interests of community and even enterprise level bureaucrats. Differing sets of books were often maintained, if at all, depending on the intended audience: Statistics Bureau; Tax Bureau; and so on.

Data collection and monitoring must remain sensitive to the ambiguities of a highly mixed land use system since this was a central and persistent feature of the lower Yangzi delta. However, it is also essential for all the various levels of government and their reporting agencies to identify and utilize the same consistently defined demographic and economic indicators, and to implement standardized methods of monitoring and reporting procedures across the entire

---

[44] Huang, P. C. C. (1990) The Peasant Family and Rural Development in the Yangzi Delta, 1350–1988. Stanford: Stanford University Press, p. 38.

region. Moreover, there needs to be a much greater level of transparency in these methods and procedures, and all of the resulting information must be made freely available. Overcoming the pervasive reluctance or inability to share information will allow researchers to presage alternative development scenarios wherein careful monitoring would indicate the most likely patterns to emerge. By highlighting significant trends, potential problems, and areas of opportunity, planning and management practitioners, and commercial interests in the lower Yangzi delta could anticipate, lobby for, and coordinate more effective responses.

However, it is also important to accept that the location of production and the functions of rural communities and central places rarely result from deliberate design. The emphasis therefore, must be upon seeking an understanding of the processes and mechanisms which underlie the patterns observed or sought after, what establishes these processes and mechanisms, and what stabilizes and reproduces them. The findings of this study suggest an alternative conceptual and analytical framework to help explain, predict, and manage the complexities of spatial economic restructuring in the lower Yangzi delta. Crucial to understanding these landscapes of transformation was an exploration of the character of locality and place. Ultimately, general conclusions about processes of transformation observed in the lower Yangzi delta, and the planning and policy formation that results, must rely upon a detailed analysis of local social, political and economic change.

ABOUT THE AUTHOR

Andrew M. Marton completed his Ph.D. in Geography in 1996 at the University of British Columbia where he was most recently a Post-Doctoral Research Fellow in the Centre for Chinese Research. He joined the East Asian Institute in May 1998. His current research includes an analysis of the changing organizational and institutional structures in China's non-urban industrial sector. He is also leading a project to examine internal migration in the broader context of rural transformation in China. He has lectured extensively on issues of urban and regional development in China and East Asia and has published numerous articles and book chapters on the subject. He is currently editing a volume titled *Rural-Urban Transformation and Development in China*.